KINDERGARTEN

101 Things to Know About READING

meow

Rhyming Words

cat
hat

Beginning Sounds

bug

Sight Words

ball

Contributing Writers: Natalie Goldstein and Anne Schreiber
Consultant: Susan A. Miller, Ed.D.

active minds

Natalie Goldstein is a freelance writer and editor for children's educational books. She has contributed to dozens of activity books, textbooks, and other workbooks for many different publishers, including McGraw Hill, Houghton Mifflin, Prentice Hall, and Scholastic. In addition, she holds a master's degree in Education.

Anne Schreiber is currently the executive vice president of FrontLine Education and contributes regularly to children's educational materials. She has been an educational consultant for many companies, including PBS Teacher Line, Scholastic Education, and Disney. In addition, she is a licensed teacher and holds a master's degree in Curriculum and Instruction from Cornell University.

Susan A. Miller, Ed.D., is a Professor Emerita of Early Childhood Education at Kutztown University of Pennsylvania. She is a columnist for Scholastic's Early Childhood Today and Parent & Child magazines. She is the consultant or writer for numerous books, including *My First Dictionary, Circle Time Activities, Problem Solving Kids, and Games, Giggles, and Giant Steps*. Dr. Miller is a frequent presenter at the National Association for the Education of Young Children Conferences and the Association for Childhood Education International.

Illustrations by George Ulrich and Nicholas Myers
Cover photography by Siede Preis Photography and Brian Warling Photography

Published by
Louis Weber, C.E.O.
Publications International, Ltd.

7373 North Cicero Avenue
Lincolnwood, Illinois 60712

Ground Floor, 59 Gloucester Place
London W1U 8JJ

Customer Service: 1-800-595-8484 or customer_service@pilbooks.com

www.myactiveminds.com

ActiveMinds® is a trademark of Publications International, Ltd., and is registered in the United States.

8 7 6 5 4 3 2 1

Manufactured in China.

ISBN-13: 978-1-4127-8330-9
ISBN-10: 1-4127-8330-5

Contents

Ready to Read

Dear Parents:

Starting school is an exciting time for kinder-gartners. They are ready for new challenges, such as learning to read and write letters, recognize words, and

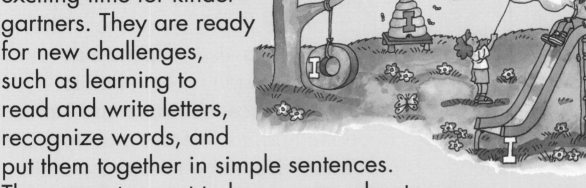

put them together in simple sentences. They seem to want to know more about every-thing! Of course you want to give your child that special head start that is so important. This workbook will help your child learn the basic skills of a vast array of reading concepts and processes—skills your child will build on in the future.

Inside this workbook, children will find 101 fun-filled reading activities right at their fingertips. Each activity focuses on a different skill and provides your child with plenty of opportunity to practice that skill. The activities are arranged in order of difficulty, beginning with the most basic skills in order to build your child's confidence as he or she goes along. They'll feel a real sense of accomplishment as they complete each page.

Every activity is clearly labeled with the skill being taught. You will find skill keys written especially for you, the parent, at the bottom of the page. These skill keys give you informa-tion about what your child is learning. Also, suggestions are provided for additional hands-on activities you may choose to do with your child. These offer fun, enjoyable opportunities to reinforce the skill being taught.

Children learn in a variety of ways. They are sure to appreciate the bright, exciting illustrations in this workbook. The pictures are not just fun—they also help visual learners develop their reading skills by giving them something to relate to. Children may also like to touch and trace the letters and words and say them out loud. Each method can be an important aid in your child's learning process. Have markers and a pencil and paper at the ready—the more practice your child gets, the better. He or she will enjoy putting these new skills to work.

Your child can tackle some of the activities independently; in other cases you will need to read the directions for your child before he or she can complete the exercise. Each activity should be fun and enough of a challenge that it will be exciting for your child. Be patient and support your child in positive ways. Let them know it's all right to take a guess or pull back if they're unsure. And, of course, celebrate their successes with them. Read every day! Reading together is fun for both of you. Learning should be an exciting and positive experience for everyone. Enjoy your time together as your child enhances his or her kindergarten reading skills.

My Name

Your name has letters in it. Say the letters in your name. The letters make the sounds in your name. Say your name. Write the letters of your name on the name tag.

Parents: If your child cannot write his or her name, write it for him or her on a separate sheet of paper. Have your child copy the name on the name tag above.

Skill: Writing child's name

Answers will vary.

Now I Know My ABCs

There are 26 letters in the alphabet. Do you know the alphabet song? Touch each letter as you sing the song or say each letter.

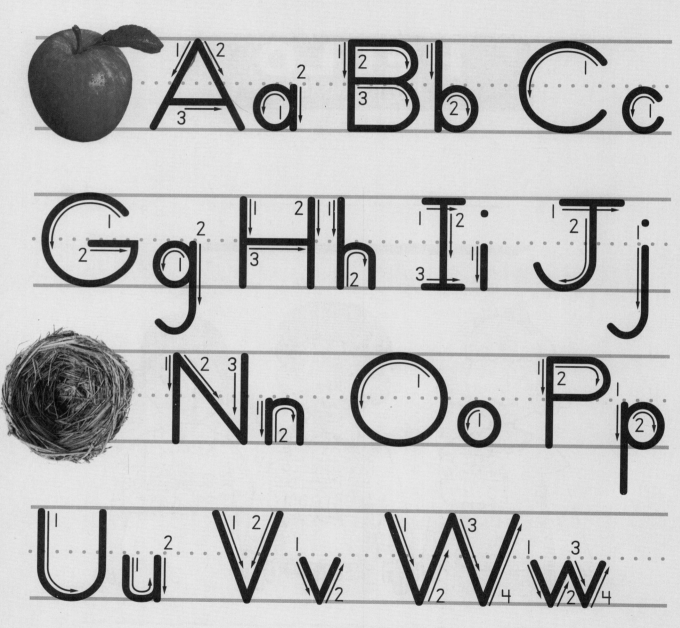

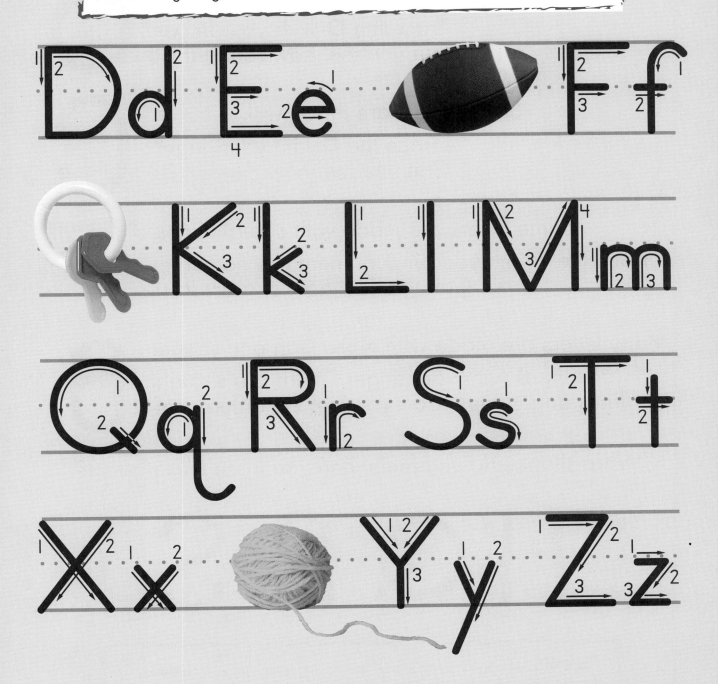

9

Alphabet Shapes

The alphabet is made up of letters. Letters have different shapes.

Some letters are made with a circle:
Trace the **O** with your finger.
Can you feel how round it is?

Some letters are made with a curve:
Trace the **C** with your finger.
Can you feel how curvy it is?

Some letters are made with straight lines:
Trace the **T** with your finger. There are no curves
at all! Can you feel how straight it is?

Many letters are made with more than one shape:
Trace the **B** with your finger. There are straight
lines and curves. Can you feel the difference?

O
C
T
B

What shapes do you feel when you trace these letters?

H Q R S

Parents: Invite your child to practice making letter shapes by drawing
them in the sand or forming them with chenille stems or yarn.

Skill: Identifying shapes in letters

Big and Small Letters

Big letters are called <u>uppercase</u> letters. Small letters are called <u>lowercase</u> letters. Write the letters on the lines.

The uppercase letters are always written between the two solid lines on the paper: **v**

Look at the different ways the lowercase letters are written: between the solid lines, below the middle line, below the bottom line.

F is uppercase. **f** is lowercase.

R is uppercase. **r** is lowercase.

G is uppercase. **g** is lowercase.

Match the uppercase letters to the lowercase letters.

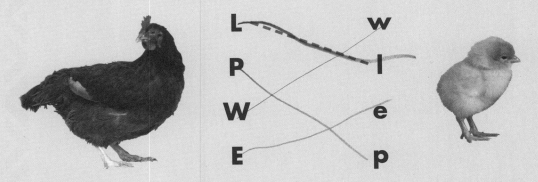

L   w

P

W   l

      e

E   p

A Is for Apple

Apple begins with the short **a** sound.
Can you say **apple**?

Trace the **A.** Then write **A.**

Trace the **a.** Then write **a.**

Animal begins with a short **a** sound. Can you draw an animal eating an apple? Awesome!

A Is also for Ape

Ape begins with the long **a** sound.
Can you say **ape**?

Apron also begins with the long **a** sound.
Can you draw an ape wearing an apron?

Parents: Together with your child, think of things that start with **a.** See if your child can tell which is the long **a** sound and which is the short **a** sound.

Skills: Saying the letter sounds of **a**; writing **A** and **a**; identifying objects that begin with the **a** sounds; distinguishing between long and short **a** sounds

Answers will vary.

B Is for Ball

Ball begins with the **b** sound.
Can you say **ball**?

Trace the **B.** Then write **B.**

Trace the **b.** Then write **b.**

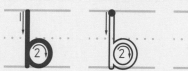

Look at the picture. Circle the things that begin with the sound of **b.**

Parents: Play "Where's the **B**?" with your child. Look around your home for objects that start with the letter **b.** Have your child write the letter **b** for each object he or she finds—uppercase **B** for big objects; lowercase **b** for small ones.

Skills: Saying the letter sound of **b**; writing **B** and **b**; identifying objects that begin with the **b** sound

14

Answers on page 122.

C Is for Cat

The letter **c** has two sounds. **Cat** begins with the hard **c** sound. Can you say **cat**?

Trace the **C.** Then write **C.**

Trace the **c.** Then write **c.**

Do you see seven **C**s hidden in this picture? They are all found in things that begin with the hard **c** sound in **cat.** Trace over each **c**, then circle it.

Skills: Saying the hard sound of **c**; writing **C** and **c**; identifying objects that begin with the hard **c** sound

Answers on page 122.

C Is also for Cereal

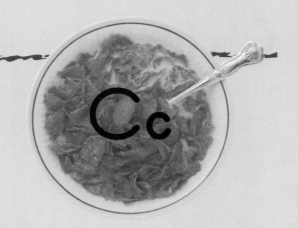

Cereal begins with the soft **c** sound. Can you say **cereal**?

Draw a picture of yourself eating your favorite cereal.

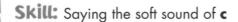

Skill: Saying the soft sound of **c**

Answers will vary.

D Is for Dog

Dog begins with the **d** sound.
Can you say **dog**?

Trace the **D.** Then write **D.**

Trace the **d.** Then write **d.**

What else begins with the sound of **d**? Connect the dots to find out.

Parents: Some children are confused by **b** and **d**. Have your child practice making these letters with lengths of play dough or other tactile materials. You may have your child do an activity called "making the bed." Write an **e** in the middle of a piece of paper. Have your child use a length of play dough to form a **b** to the left and a **d** to the right. Point out that the resulting word, **bed,** is shaped like a bed. The **b** and the **d** are its head and foot.

Skills: Saying the letter sound of **d**; writing **D** and **d**; identifying objects that begin with the **d** sound

Answers on page 122.

E Is for Egg and E-mail

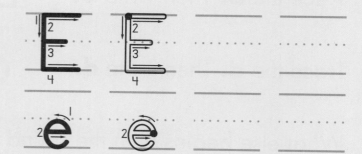

The letter **e** has two sounds. **Egg** begins with the short **e** sound. Can you say **egg**?

Trace the **E.** Then write **E.**

Trace the **e.** Then write **e.**

Some things in this egg carton do not begin with the short **e** sound. Circle the objects that start with the short **e** sound. Make an **X** through everything that does not begin with the short **e** sound.

E-mail begins with the long **e** sound. Can you say **e-mail**? To whom would you like to send an e-mail? What would you say?

Skills: Saying the letter sounds of **e**; writing **E** and **e**; identifying objects that begin with the **e** sounds; distinguishing between long and short **e** sounds

18

Answers on page 122.

F Is for Fish

Fish begins with the **f** sound.
Can you say **fish**?

Trace the **F.** Then write **F.**

Trace the **f.** Then write **f.**

Gone Fishing

Look what's floating in this pond! Find the things that begin with the sound of **f.** Say the words out loud. Draw a line to connect them to the fishing pole.

Parents: Go fishing for magnetic alphabet letters with a magnet on a string. For each "fish" your child catches, have him or her say the letter and name something that begins with that letter.

Skills: Saying the letter sound of **f**; writing **F** and **f**; identifying objects that begin with the **f** sound

Answers on page 122.

G Is for Goat and Giraffe

The letter **g** has two sounds. **Goat** begins with the hard **g** sound. Can you say **goat**?

Trace the **G.** Then write **G.**

  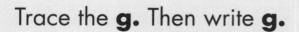

Trace the **g.** Then write **g.**

Giraffe begins with the soft **g** sound. Can you say **giraffe**? Draw a giraffe here.

Ready, Set, Go!

The goose won the race. Help her select a prize that begins with the hard sound of **g.**

The giraffe came in second place. His prize begins with the soft sound of **g.** What did he win?

The goat finished third. Which prize did he win? It starts with the hard sound of **g.**

Skills: Saying the letter sounds of **g**; writing **G** and **g**; identifying objects that begin with the **g** sound; identifying soft and hard sounds of **g**

Answers on page 122.

H Is for Hat

Hat begins with the **h** sound.
Can you say **hat**?

Trace the **H.** Then write **H.**

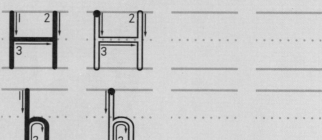

Trace the **h.** Then write **h.**

Hand It Over

Which hands hold something that begins with the **h** sound?
Say the words out loud. Circle the hands holding objects that
begin with the **h** sound.

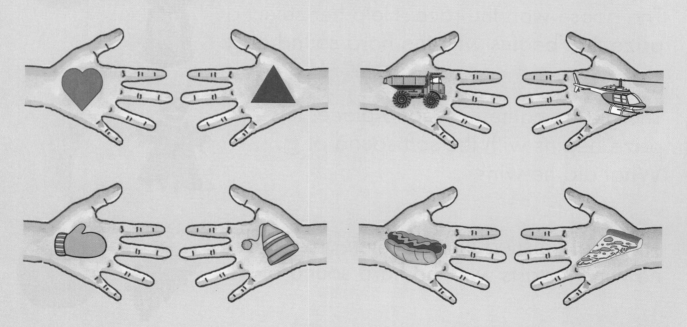

> **Skills:** Saying the letter sound of **h**; writing **H** and **h**; identifying objects that
> begin with the **h** sound

Answers on page 122.

I Is for Igloo and Ice Cream

The letter **i** has two sounds. **Igloo** begins with the short **i** sound. Can you say **igloo**?

Trace the I. Then write I.

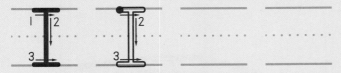

Trace the **i.** Then write **i.**

Draw an icky insect inside this igloo.

Ice cream begins with the long **i** sound. Can you say **ice cream**? Draw an ice cream cone with your favorite ice cream flavors and toppings.

Skills: Saying the letter sounds of **i**; writing I and **i**; identifying objects that begin with the **i** sounds; distinguishing between long and short **i** sounds

Answers will vary.

J Is for Jar

Jar begins with the j sound. Can you say **jar**?

Trace the J. Then write J.

Trace the j. Then write j.

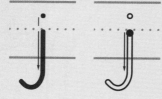

Fill this jar with pictures of things that begin with the sound of j. How about jellybeans? jacks? a juice box? What other things can you think of?

Parents: Give your child a stack of index cards with a different letter on each card. Have him or her search for an object that begins with a particular letter and place the correct letter card on it.

Skills: Saying the letter sound of j; writing J and j; identifying objects that begin with the j sound

Answers will vary.

K Is for Kite

Kite begins with the **k** sound.
Can you say **kite**?

Trace the **K.** Then write **K.**

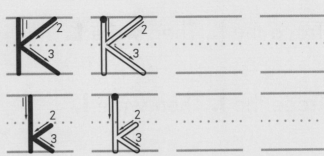

Trace the **k.** Then write **k.**

Key begins with the sound of **k.** Kyle is locked out of his house. Follow the **K**s to help him use his key to open the door. Color this path.

```
W  R  G  Z  L  P  T  B
P  B  Y  V  R  T  C  D
X  V  F  T  Y  L  H  V
K  Z  P  W  T  Y  R  W
C  K  T  K  K  Z  B  F
R  F  K  H  P  K  J  V
J  Y  H  V  F  K  D  C
G  T  J  P  M  L  K  K
Y  G  L  C  N  Q  R  S
```

Skills: Saying the letter sound of **k**; writing **K** and **k**; identifying the letter **k**

L Is for Lion

Lion begins with the **l** sound.
Can you say **lion**?

Trace the **L.** Then write **L.**

Trace the **l.** Then write **l.**

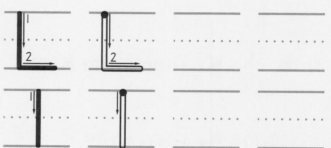

The lion has lost his lollipop. Help him find his lollipop and three more foods that begin with the sound of **l.** Circle these foods.

Skills: Saying the letter sound of **l**; writing **L** and **l**; identifying objects that begin with the **l** sound

Answers on page 122.

M Is for Mouse

Mm

Mouse begins with the **m** sound.
Can you say **mouse**?

Trace the **M.** Then write **M.**

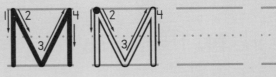

Trace the **m.** Then write **m.**

Mmmmmm . . . let's see. What else starts with **m**? Color the shapes that have the letter **M.** Leave the other shapes blank, or color them a different color.

Skills: Saying the letter sound of **m**; writing **M** and **m**; identifying the letter **m**

Answers on page 122.

N Is for Nut

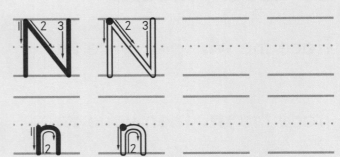

Nut begins with the **n** sound.
Can you say **nut**?

Trace the **N.** Then write **N.**

Trace the **n.** Then write **n.**

Write an **n** to answer each riddle.

I am on your face. I smell things.

I am your ___ose.

You hammer me. I hold wood together.

I am a ___ail.

I am in a tree. Birds live in me.

I am a ___est.

You eat me. You find me in soup.

I am a ___oodle.

Parents: Give your child a crayon and a sheet of paper. Ask him or her to write the letter **n.** Then have your child turn the letter into something that begins with the letter **n.**

Skills: Saying the letter sound of **n**; writing **N** and **n**; adding a specific letter to complete a word

Answers on page 123.

O Is for Octopus

The letter **o** has two sounds. **Octopus** begins with the short **o** sound. Can you say **octopus**?

Trace the **O.** Then write **O.**

Trace the **o.** Then write **o.**

Oscar is hungry! Help him choose toppings for his pizza. Say the names of the toppings out loud. Circle the foods that begin with the short sound of **o.**

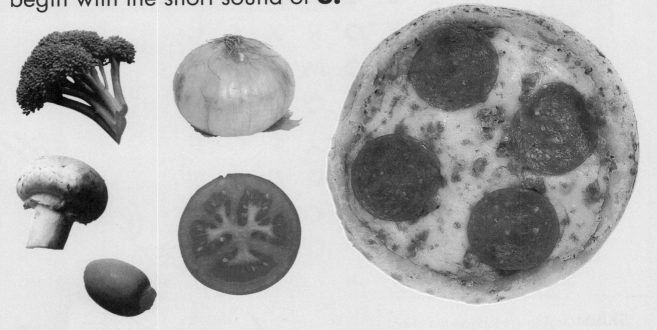

Skills: Saying the short sound of **o**; writing **O** and **o**; identifying objects that begin with the short **o** sound; identifying the letter **o**

Answers on page 123.

O Is also for Ocean

Ocean begins with the long **o** sound. Can you say **ocean**?

Help Owen follow the path of **O**s over to the ocean. Color this path.

Owen

```
W  F  G  Z  L  P  T  B
O  O  H  V  F  Y  D  C
G  T  O  F  M  P  B  P
Y  G  O  K  N  Q  R  N
P  J  O  C  N  M  F  V
P  B  Y  O  R  X  C  K
X  V  F  O  M  P  H  T
K  Z  C  S  O  O  R  S
D  Y  H  V  J  L  O  P
V  G  T  R  D  C  O  N
P  N  R  Z  C  Y  M  O
```

Skills: Saying the long sound of **o**; identifying the letter **o**

Answers on page 123.

P Is for Pig

Pig begins with the **p** sound.
Can you say **pig**?

Trace the **P.** Then write **P.**

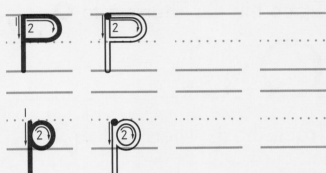

Trace the **p.** Then write **p.**

The Princess and the P

Palace, pony, princess, pig, pears, platter, penguins, present, and **prince** all begin with the sound of **p.** Color them in.

Skills: Saying the letter sound of **p**; writing **P** and **p**; identifying objects that begin with the **p** sound

Answers on page 123.

Q Is for Queen

Queen begins with the **q** sound.
Can you say **queen**?

Trace the **Q.** Then write **Q.**

Trace the **q**. Then write **q**.

The queen has a question. How can she decorate her quilt? Practice writing **Q** and **q** in each square of the quilt.

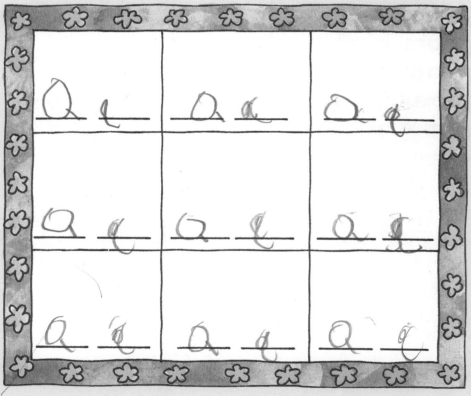

Skills: Saying the letter sound of **q**; writing **Q** and **q**

Answers on page 123.

R Is for Rabbit

Rabbit begins with the **r** sound.
Can you say **rabbit**?

Trace the **R.** Then write **R.**

Trace the **r.** Then write **r.**

Rooster, rabbit, rhinoceros, and **rat** all start with the sound of **r.** Can you draw a silly creature that has parts of some of these animals?

Parents: Write an uppercase and a lowercase **r** on separate index cards nine or ten times. Write other letters on other cards. Make a maze of stepping stones around the room. Challenge your child to make his or her way across the room, stepping only on the cards with the letter **r.**

Skills: Saying the letter sound of **r**; writing **R** and **r**; identifying words that begin with the **r** sound

Answers will vary.

S Is for Sock

Sock begins with the **s** sound.
Can you say **sock**?

Trace the **S.** Then write **S.**

Trace the **s.** Then write **s.**

Soup's On!

Find and circle the **S**s
in this bowl of
alphabet soup.

Skills: Saying the letter sound of **s**; writing **S**
and **s**; identifying the letter **s**

Answers on page 123.

T Is for Top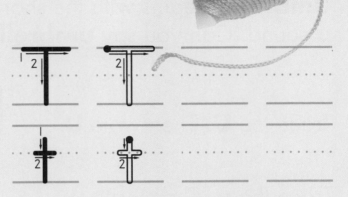

Top begins with the **t** sound.
Can you say **top**?

Trace the **T.** Then write **T.**

Trace the **t.** Then write **t.**

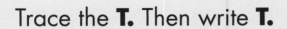

Make an X through the pictures that begin with the sound of **t.**
Can you get a tic-tac-toe?

Parents: When driving your child to school, play the license plate game.
Have your child search for a specific letter on the license plates of passing cars.

Skills: Saying the letter sound of **t**; writing **T** and **t**; identifying objects that
begin with the **t** sound

Answers on page 123.

U Is for Umbrella

The letter **u** has two sounds.
Umbrella begins with the short
u sound. Can you say **umbrella**?

Trace the **U.** Then write **U.**

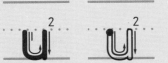

Trace the **u.** Then write **u.**

Uh-oh! This ugly duckling got caught in a rainstorm with an upside-down umbrella. It's easy to see why she's unhappy! Draw a happy duckling next to her.

U Is also for Uniform

Uniform starts with the long **u** sound.
Can you say **uniform**?

Firefighters, police officers, soldiers, and more all wear uniforms to work. Circle the people wearing a uniform.

Skills: Saying the letter sounds of **u**; writing **U** and **u**; identifying objects that begin with the **u** sounds; distinguishing between long and short **u** sounds

Answers on page 123.

V Is for Van

Van begins with the **v** sound.
Can you say **van**?

Trace the **V.** Then write **V.**

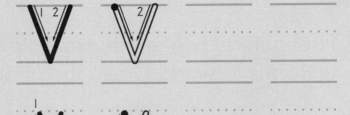

Trace the **v.** Then write **v.**

Violet sent her friends gifts that start with the sound of **v.**
Which presents start with the **v** sound? Say the words out
loud. Circle the ones that start with the **v** sound.

Skills: Saying the letter sound of **v**; writing **V** and **v**;
identifying objects that begin with the **v** sound

Answers on page 123.

W Is for Wagon

Wagon begins with the **w** sound.
Can you say **wagon**?

Trace the **W.** Then write **W.**

Trace the **w.** Then write **w.**

Look at the picture. Circle
the seven things that begin
with the sound of **w.**

Parents: In nice weather, your child may practice writing letters by "painting" them with water on a sidewalk or driveway using a large paintbrush.

Skills: Saying the letter sound of **w**; writing **W** and **w**; identifying objects that begin with the **w** sound

Answers on page 123.

X Is for X-ray

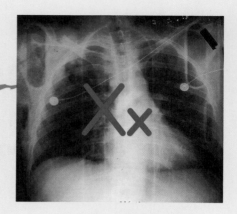

X-ray begins with the **x** sound. Can you say **x-ray**?

Trace the **X.** Then write **X.**

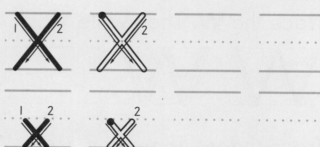

Trace the **x.** Then write **x.**

Most words do not begin with **x.** The **x** is usually found in the middle or at the end of the word.

Say the words that describe what is in the picture. Do you hear the **x** sound?

Box

Exit

X Marks the Spot

Follow the **X**s to uncover the treasure. Color the path that connects the pirate and the treasure chest. When you find the treasure, say, "X marks the spot!"

```
X  X  X  X  L  Z  S  B  M  C
K  Z  P  X  S  R  R  W  K  Q
C  R  T  Y  X  Z  B  N  J  L
P  B  N  J  W  X  C  D  G  M
J  Y  H  V  F  X  D  C  K  N
P  J  Y  B  K  X  X  V  T  R
G  T  J  D  M  P  B  X  X  R
C  Z  P  N  T  Y  R  W  S  X
R  F  K  Q  P  K  J  V  B  X
```

Skills: Saying the letter sound of **x**; writing **X** and **x**; identifying the letter **x**

Y Is for Yarn

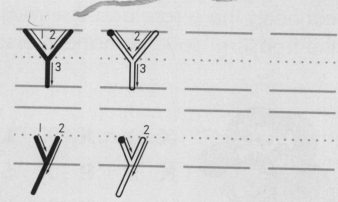

Yarn begins with the **y** sound.
Can you say **yarn**?

Trace the **Y.** Then write **Y.**

Trace the **y.** Then write **y.**

Yikes! These balls of yarn are all tangled up. Which ball of yarn leads to the blue yo-yo? Write the number here. ____

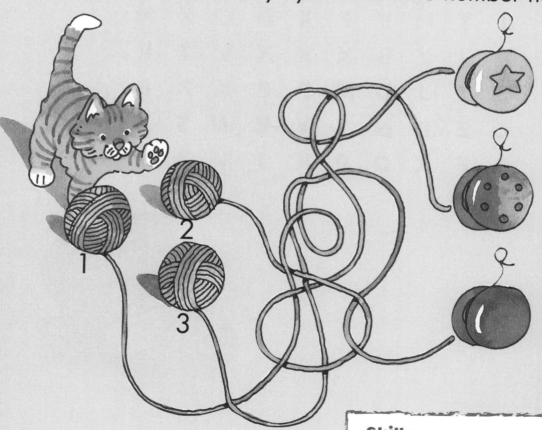

Skills: Saying the letter sound of **y**; writing **Y** and **y**

Answers on page 123.

Z Is for Zipper

Zipper begins with the **z** sound.
Can you say **zipper**?

Trace the **Z**. Then write **Z**.

Trace the **z**. Then write **z**.

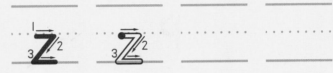

At the Zoo

Each zebra has a **z** hidden in its stripes. Find and circle each **z**.

Parents: Trace the different letters of the alphabet with your finger on your child's back. See if he or she can guess what letter you are tracing.

Skills: Saying the letter sound of **z**; writing **Z** and **z**; identifying the letter **z**

Answers on page 123.

Letter Match

Draw a line from the letter to the picture that begins with that letter sound.

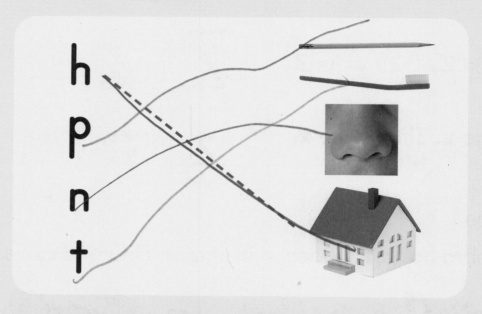

What Comes Next?

Fill in the blanks with the letter that comes next.

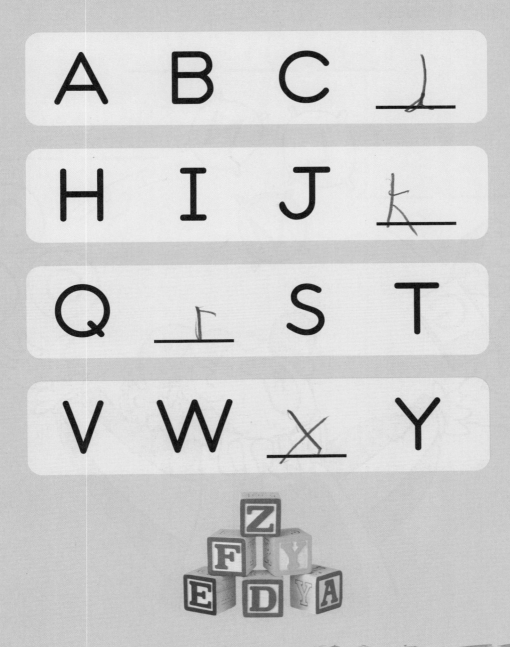

A B C _D_

H I J _K_

Q _R_ S T

V W _X_ Y

Parents: Under your supervision, have your child cut out the letters of his or her name from a magazine. Place the letters in a bowl and have your child pull out one letter at a time. Ask your child to read each letter aloud as he or she places them in the correct order to spell his or her name.

Skills: Writing letters; identifying the order of the letters of the alphabet

Answers on page 124.

ABC Order

These letters are all mixed up. Can you put them in alphabetical order?

Answers on page 124.

Letter Scramble

Draw a line connecting the uppercase letter to the lowercase letter that matches it.

Parents: For additional practice, play a matching game. On one index card, write an uppercase letter. On a second card, write the corresponding lowercase letter. Do this for as many letters as you want, and invite your child to match the letters together in pairs.

Skill: Matching uppercase letters to their corresponding lowercase letters

_lock

_lag

_eacher

_ish

_esk

ru_b

boo_k

Beginning and Ending Sounds

Say the name of each picture. Write the beginning or ending sound on each line.

doo___

han___

fee___

penci___

Skills: Recognizing sounds; writing letters

Answers on page 124.

Mail Call!

The mail carrier is delivering letters to each house on the block. Draw a line from each letter to the mailbox in which it belongs. Write the letter on the line to complete the word.

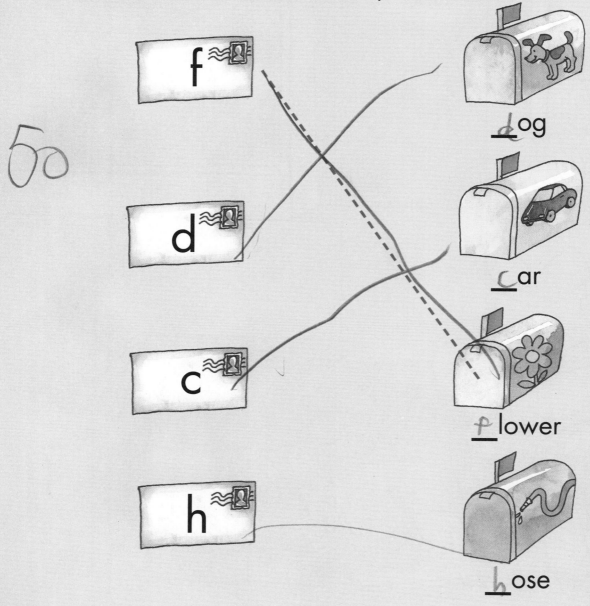

__d__og

__c__ar

__f__lower

__h__ose

Parents: Set up six shoe boxes or other small boxes, each labeled with a letter. Cut several pictures from magazines. Have your child identify each picture and "mail" it to the box with the same letter as the beginning sound.

Skills: Identifying beginning and ending sounds; writing letters

Answers on page 124.

A, E, I, O, and U (and sometimes Y)

There are five <u>vowels</u> in the alphabet. They are **a, e, i, o,** and **u.** Every word has at least one vowel. Sometimes **y** is a vowel, as in the word **my** or **family.**

Color the boxes that have vowels. What do you see?

My doll

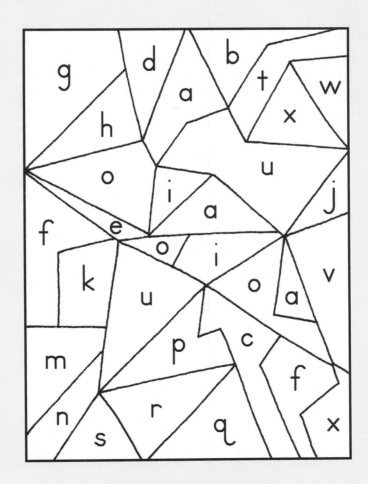

Skill: Recognizing vowels

51

Answers on

Short A, Long A

Apple, animal, and **ant** begin with the short **a** sound. Short **a** is also heard in the middle of **cat, dad,** and **van.** Say these words out loud. Do you hear the short **a**?

Andy's Dad Drives a Van

Which vans carry an item with the short **a** sound in the middle? Circle them.

Ape, apron, and **age** begin with the long **a** sound. Long **a** is also heard in the middle of **rake, game,** and **page.**

Play a Game with Long **A**!

Trace your way through the maze, following the pictures that have the long **a** sound in the middle.

Skills: Recognizing the letter **a**; recognizing long **a** and short **a** sounds

Answers on page 124.

Short E, Long E

Egg, elephant, and **elbow** begin with the short **e** sound.
Short **e** is also heard in the middle of **leg, beg,** and **peg.**
Say these words out loud. Do you hear the short **e**?

The Messy Bedroom

Check out Ben's messy bedroom. Circle the things that have
the short **e** sound in the middle.

Eagle, each, and **even** begin with the long **e** sound. Long **e** is also heard in the middle of **teeth, queen,** and **meat.**

The Wheel of Long E

Which pictures on this wheel have the long **e** sound? Say the words out loud. Circle the pictures that have the long **e** sound.

Skill: Recognizing long **e** and short **e** sounds

Answers on page 124.

Short I, Long I

Igloo, inch, and **ink** begin with the short **i** sound. Short **i** is also heard in the middle of **pig, fish,** and **chin.** Say these words out loud. Do you hear the short **i**?

Brick by Brick

Build a brick wall with words with short **i** sounds. Copy each word with a short **i** sound in the middle onto its own brick.

six   bag   ship   bed   cup   pig   chick

Ice, iron, and **ivy** begin with the long **i** sound. Long **i** is also heard in the middle of **vine, tire,** and **kite.**

I Spy

Can you spy the letter I? Circle it every time you see it in the picture below.

Skills: Writing letters; recognizing the letter **i**; recognizing long **i** and short **i** sounds

Answers on page 124.

Short O, Long O

Octopus, olive, and **on** begin with the short **o** sound. Short **o** is also heard in the middle of **dot, top,** and **fox.** Say these words out loud. Do you hear the short **o**?

Connect the Dots

Connect the dots to find something else that has the short **o** sound in the middle.

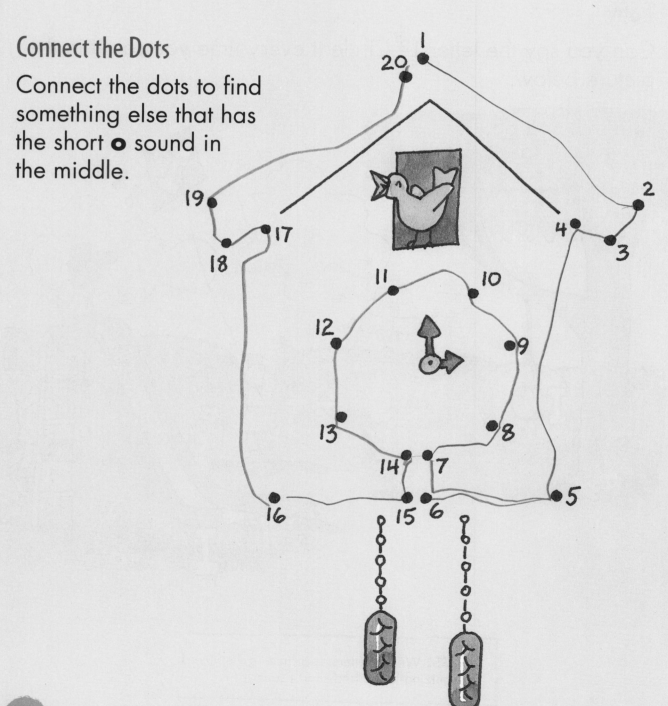

Over, oval, and **only** begin with the long **o** sound. Long **o** is also heard in the middle of **rope, coat,** and **bowl.**

It's Only a Joke

To answer these riddles, think of a word with the long **o** sound in the middle. Write the word.

What falls in winter but never gets hurt?

_____

. . . .

_____

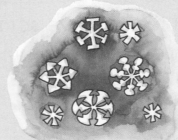

What can you put in a bucket of water to make it lighter?

_____

. . . .

_____

What is it that even the most careful people overlook? Their

_____

. . . .

_____

> **Skills:** Recognizing long **o** and short **o** sounds; writing words

Short U, Long U

Umbrella, under, and **up** begin with the short **u** sound. Short **u** is also heard in the middle of **cup, gum,** and **rub.** Say these words out loud. Do you hear the short **u**?

Bubbles of Fun

These bubbles are floating every which way. If you're lucky, you'll catch them! Have some fun and draw these things that have the short **u** sound in the middle.

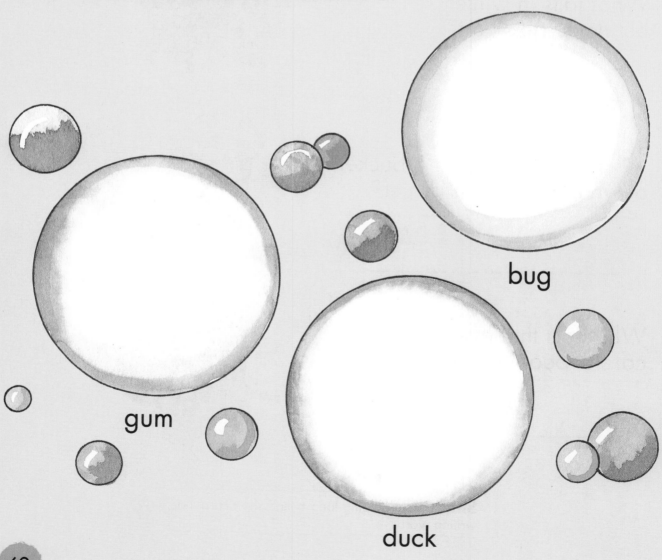

bug

gum

duck

Unicorn, useful, and **uniform** begin with the long **u** sound. Long **u** is also heard in **glue, blue,** and **fruit.**

Put Your Super Skills to Good Use

The universe is filled with things that have the long **u** sound. Draw yourself in a spacesuit on the planet Uranus.

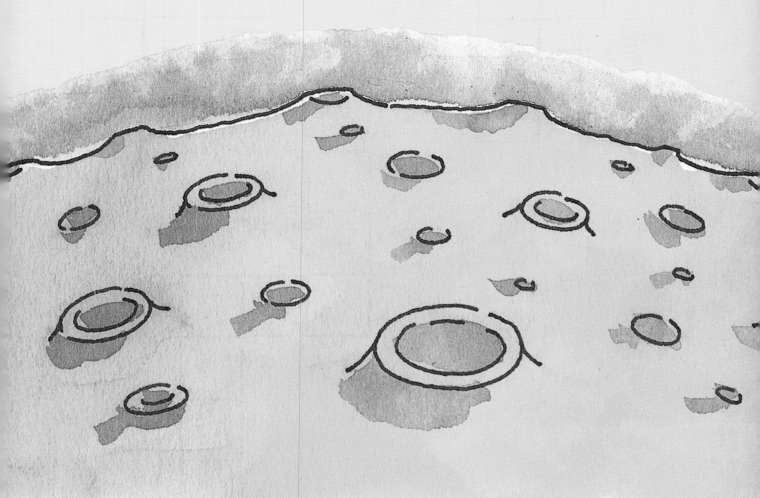

Skill: Recognizing long **u** and short **u** sounds

Short Vowel Puzzles

Look at the pictures. Write the words in the puzzle squares.

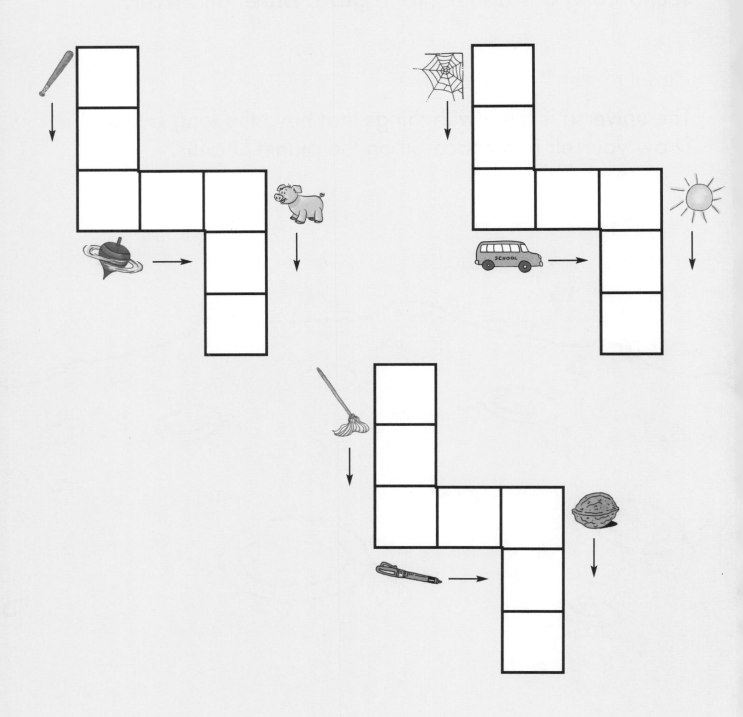

Answers on page 125.

Missing A

Say the name of each object. Write the missing short vowel to complete the word.

f_n

c_t

b_g

m_p

These words have the short **a** sound in the middle. Put the sounds together to read the word. Say it out loud! In the example, **c+a+t** spells **cat**.

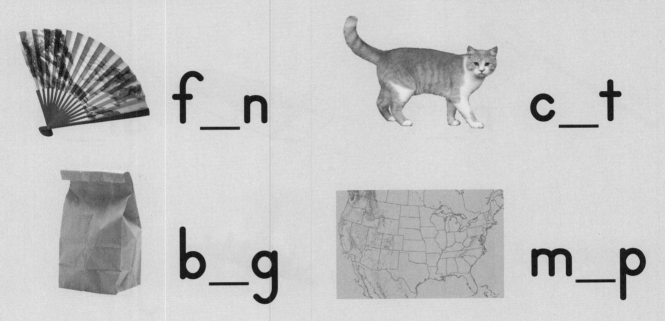

c+a+t

cat

c+a+p

t+a+p

t+a+b

Skills: Writing **a**; putting sounds together to read words

Answers on page 125.

Missing E

Say the name of each object. Write the missing short vowel to complete the word.

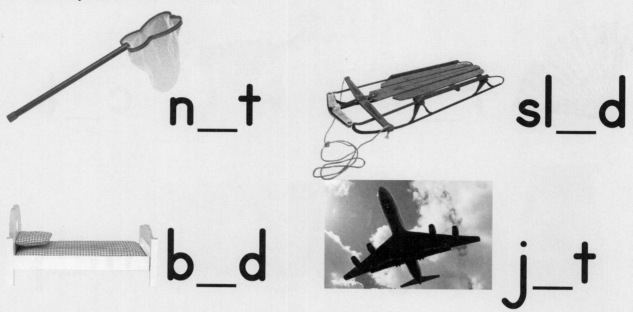

n_t

sl_d

b_d

j_t

These words have the short **e** sound in the middle. Put the sounds together to read the word. Say it out loud! In the example, **n+e+t** spells **net**.

n+e+t

net

r+e+d   p+e+n   w+e+t

Skills: Writing **e**; putting sounds together to read words

Answers on page 125.

Missing I

Say the name of each object. Write the missing short vowel to complete the word.

p_g

f__sh

r_ng

w_g

These words have the short **i** sound in the middle. Put the sounds together to read the word. Say it out loud! In the example, **p+i+g** spells **pig**.

p+i+g

pig

d+i+d

w+i+n

b+i+t

Skills: Writing **i**; putting sounds together to read words

Answers on page 125.

Missing O

Say the name of each object. Write the missing short vowel to complete the word.

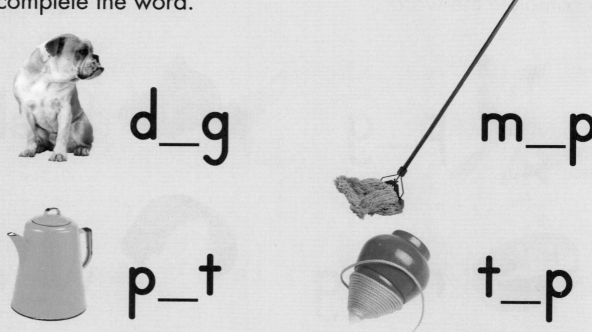

d_g

m_p

p_t

t_p

These words have the short **o** sound in the middle. Put the sounds together to read the word. Say it out loud! In the example, **d+o+g** spells **dog**.

d+o+g

dog

h+o+t

l+o+g

d+o+t

Skills: Writing **o**; putting sounds together to read words

Answers on page 125.

Missing U

Say the name of each object. Write the missing short vowel to complete the word.

s_n

b_g

dr_m

s_b

These words have the short **u** sound in the middle. Put the sounds together to read the word. Say it out loud! In the example, **s+u+n** spells **sun**.

s+u+n

sun

m+u+d

h+u+g

b+u+n

Skills: Writing **u**; putting sounds together to read words

Answers on page 125.

You Can Spell!

To spell each word, write the letter sounds you hear. The first word is done for you.

bag

Wacky Word Search

Find the short vowel words hidden in the puzzle below. Circle them. The words go across and up-and-down. Cross out each word in the word bank as you find it.

~~bun~~ ~~get~~ ~~hop~~ ~~sad~~ ~~win~~

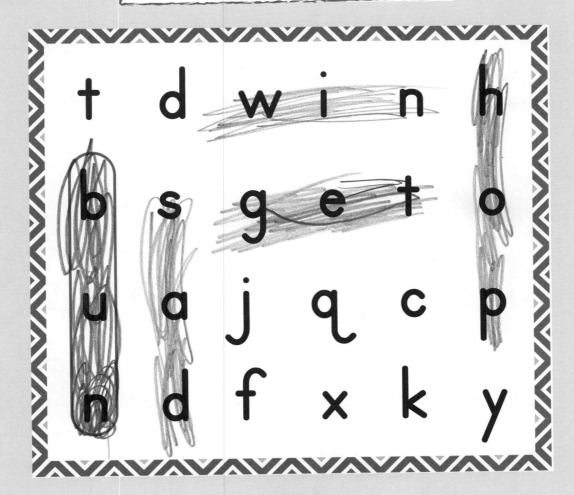

Step Toward Spelling

Say the word **bus.** Do you hear the **b** sound at the beginning of **bus**? Do you hear the **s** sound at the end?

Spell **bus.** ___ U ___

Say the name of each picture out loud. Write down the missing letter you hear in each word.

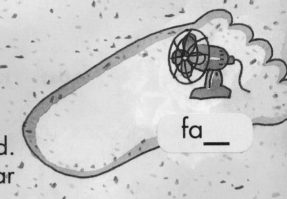

fa__

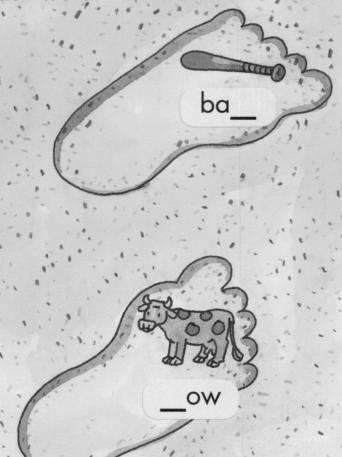

ba__

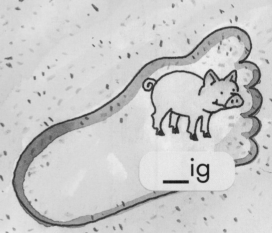

__ig

__ow

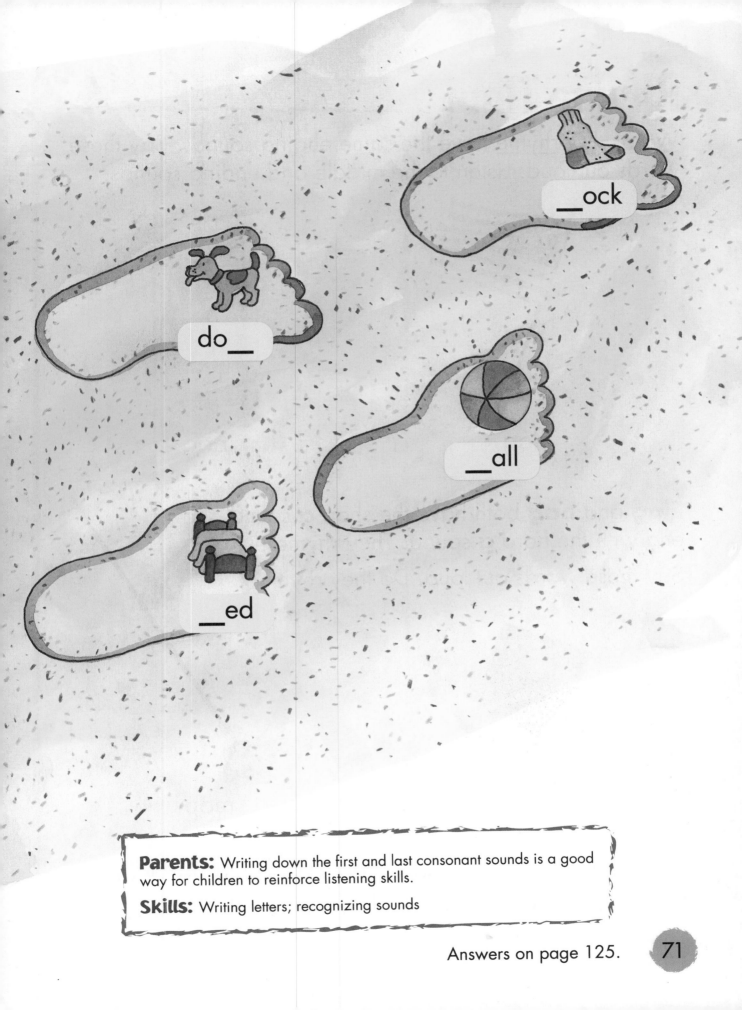

__ock

do__

__all

__ed

Answers on page 125.

Rhyme Time

Words that <u>rhyme</u> have the same ending sounds. Say these words out loud. Listen to the middle and ending sounds.

flag

bag

Flag and **bag** both have the short **a** sound and end with the hard **g** sound. They rhyme!

Say these words out loud. Do they rhyme?

box

mop

Box and **mop** do not rhyme. They both have the short **o** sound, but the ending sounds are different.

Look at the picture. Say the word out loud. Circle the word that rhymes.

sled

bed   food

bug

hug   fun

mouse

nose   house

cow

now   not

ball

tall   bag

sink

wink   sing

Skill: Recognizing rhyming words

Word Families

You can put some words into groups. Groups make it easy to learn new words. These groups are called <u>word families.</u> Words in a word family have the same ending. For example, **cat, hat,** and **fat** are part of the **at** word family.

Can you think of more words to fit in each of these word families? Write the beginning letters on each line. Some examples are done for you.

an	**ed**	**it**	**op**	**ug**
can	led	hit	pop	hug
fan	wed	quit	drop	tug
___an	___ed	___it	___op	___ug
___an	___ed	___it	___op	___ug

Parents: Grouping words together into families can make it easier for children to learn new words. Seeing that **c+at** spells **cat,** for instance, may help them figure out that **h+at** spells **hat.**

Skills: Recognizing rhyming words; identifying word families; writing letters

Answers will vary.

A Fat Cat

Adding different letters in front of the word ending **at** makes different words.

Write the words. Say them out loud.

b+at=_____

c+at=_____

f+at=_____

h+at=_____

p+at=_____

r+at=_____

Can you spell these **at** words? Now write them below.

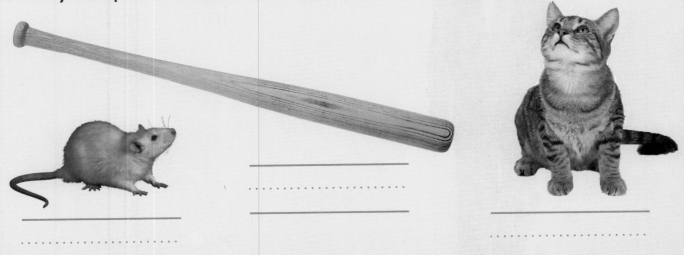

Answers on page 126.

The Man Ran

You can put different letters in front of the word ending **an.** Adding different letters makes different words.

Look at the picture. Say the word. Circle the **an** word that matches the picture.

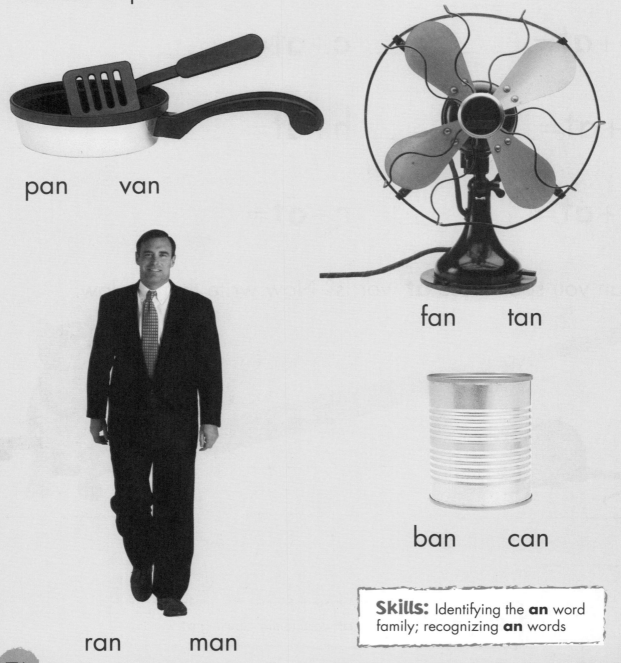

pan   van

fan   tan

ban   can

ran   man

Answers on page 126.

Ten Men and a Hen

You can put different letters in front of the word ending **en.**
Adding different letters makes different words.

Circle the word that answers the riddle. Write it in the blank.

I am a chicken. I lay eggs.

I am a _____

pen   hen

I am a number. I come after the number nine.

I am number _____

ten   when

I am more than one man.

I am a group of _____

then   men

Skills: Identifying the **en** word
family; spelling **en** words

Answers on page 126.

The Pet Is Wet

You can put different letters in front of the word ending **et.**
Adding different letters makes different words.

Read the sentences. Circle the word
that rhymes with the underlined word.
Write it in the blank.

I take my <u>pet</u> to visit the _____

vet   bed

I have not <u>yet</u> flown in a _____

kite   jet

I always get <u>wet</u> when I fish with a _____

wag   net

Skills: Identifying the **et** word family; spelling **et** words

Answers on page 126.

The Pin Is Thin

Adding different letters in front of the word ending **in** makes different words.

Draw a **grin** on this **thin** face. Draw an arrow that points to his **chin.** Draw some freckles on his **skin.**

Answers will vary.

The Ring Is the Thing

Adding different letters in front of the word ending **ing** makes different words.

Circle the word that answers the riddle. Write it in the blank.

I am pretty. You wear me on your finger.

I am a _____

ring   wing

I wear a crown. I live in a castle.

I am a _____

ping   king

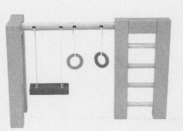

You sit on me. You move me back and forth.

I am a _____

swing   ding

Skills: Identifying the **ing** word family; spelling **ing** words

Answers on page 126.

Hop, Bop, 'n Pop

You can put different letters in front of the word ending **op.**
Adding different letters makes different words.

Write the words. Say them out loud.

b+op=_____   c+op=_____

h+op=_____   m+op=_____

p+op=_____

Stop is part of the **op** family. Draw a stop sign in the box at right. (Hint: A stop sign has eight sides.)

Don't Block the Clock

Adding different letters in front of the word ending **ock** makes different words.

Draw a line to connect the word with the picture it describes.

block

rock

clock

lock

sock

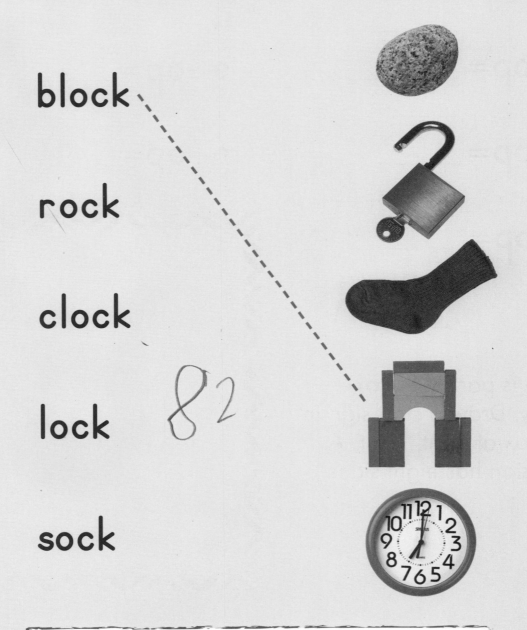

82

Answers on page 126.

A Bug in a Rug

You can put different letters in front of the word ending **ug.**
Adding different letters makes different words.

Look at the pictures. Say the word out loud.
Can you tell what letter comes first?
Write it on the line.

__ug

__ug

__ug

__ug

Fun in the Sun

Adding different letters in front of the word ending **un** makes different words.

Write the words. Say them out loud.

b+un= _____

r+un= _____

s+un= _____

Fun and **sun** are part of the **un** word family. Have fun in the sun! Draw a picture of yourself having fun in the sun.

Skills: Identifying the **un** word family; spelling **un** words

Answers on page 126.

Family Friends

Underline the words in each word family. Cross out the sound from the word bank as you find it. The first one is done for you.

ed   at   ~~ock~~   op

Hickory dickory <u>dock</u>.
The mouse ran up the <u>clock</u>.

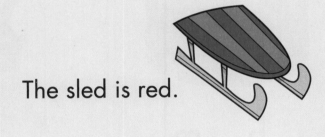

The sled is red.

The cop said stop.

There's a fat rat on the mat.

Parents: Kids love to make rhymes. Play a rhyming game with your child in which you say a word out loud and ask him or her to think of a word that rhymes.

Skills: Recognizing rhyming words; identifying word families

What's at the End?

Say the name of each picture. Listen to the letter sound you hear at the end of each word.

Circle the letter of the ending sound.

b m

d f

k g

n s

n t

Skill: Identifying ending sounds

Answers on page 126.

Great Endings

Say the words below. Write the ending letter sound you hear.

elephan__

skun__

lio__

tige__

Skill: Identifying ending sounds

Shh! Silent e

Some words end in **e.** But you do not say the **e** sound and you do not hear it. This is a <u>silent **e.**</u>

Look at each picture. Say the word out loud. Write the letter sounds you hear. The silent **e** at the end is done for you.

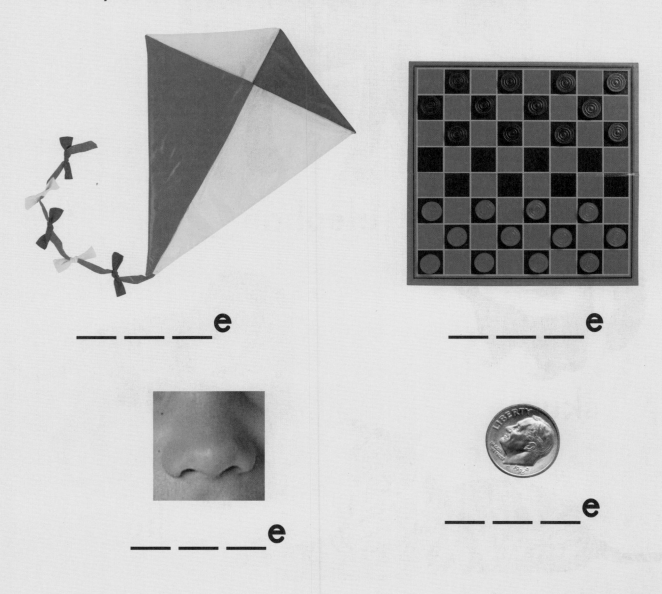

___ ___ ___ **e**

___ ___ ___ **e**

___ ___ ___ **e**

___ ___ ___ **e**

Answers on page 126.

Words to Know

A, an, and **the** are found in many sentences. They are called <u>sight words.</u> They are words to know when you see them. Circle **a, an,** and **the** every time you see them in the story below.

A boy has an olive pizza. He brings the pizza to a house. The boy eats the pizza. He has a friend. His friend eats the pizza too. They eat an awesome meal.

Parents: Practicing <u>sight words</u> such as these with your child will make a dramatic difference as they learn to read. Have your child point them out in books and nursery rhymes.

Skill: Identifying sight words **a, an, the**

He, She, It, and They

Sometimes a person or thing is called something else. **He, she, it,** and **they** can take the place of other words.

The **balloon** is green. If we don't say balloon, we can say **it. It** is green. **It** means the same as **balloon** in this sentence.

In the sentences below, underline the word that takes the place of another word. The first one is done for you.

The **girl** is dancing.
<u>She</u> is dancing.

The **children** are making music. They are making music.

The **boy** is marching.
He is marching.

The **apple** is red.
It is red.

Parents: These words are called <u>pronouns.</u> A pronoun stands for a person or thing.

Skill: Identifying pronouns **he, she, it, they**

Answers on page 126.

I, You, and We

I, **you,** and **we** describe people.

_____

My name is _____. **I** am _____ years old.

Instead of saying your name again, you can say **I.**

Now, pretend you are talking to your best friend. You might say, "**I** am hungry. Are **you** hungry?"

To ask your mom and dad for a snack for you and your friend, you might say, "**We** are hungry."

If you like this snack, write **I** in the blank. If you and your friend like it, write **we.** If you do not like it, put an **X** on the food!

_____ like apples.

_____ like cookies.

_____ like crackers.

_____ like carrots.

_____ like popcorn.

_____ like Popsicles.

Parents: I, you, and **we** are <u>pronouns.</u> They stand for a person or people.
Skills: Identifying and writing pronouns **I, you, we**

Words that Work

Some words work hard in a sentence. They tell you a lot. They tell you about other words in the sentence.

| at | in | on | to | for | from | off |

Copy the working word onto the line.

I take a bath **at** bathtime. _____

The popcorn is **in** the bowl. _____

The bird is **on** the branch. _____

The ambulance brings sick people **to** the hospital. _____

The baker has bread **for** you. _____

She took the candy **from** the box. _____

The rocks fell **off** the truck. _____

Ready, Set, Go!

Some words describe things you <u>do</u>.
They are called <u>action words</u>.

Julia jumps.

Jumps is an action word. It tells what Julia does.

Look at the picture. What is happening? Circle the action word that goes with the picture.

shoes   red   walk

see   eyes   eyebrows

pen   write   paper

boy   dance   pants

Parents: Action words are <u>verbs.</u>
Skill: Identifying action words

94

Answers on page 127.

Acting Up

Look at the picture. Read the sentence. Underline the action word that tells what something does in each sentence. The first one is done for you.

The goose <u>hugs</u> the giraffe.

The monster runs.

The cats eat.

The fish swims.

Skill: Identifying action words

Answers on page 127.

The Name Game

Many words are the names of things. These are called <u>naming words.</u>

Match the picture with the word that names it.
Draw a line from the picture to its naming word.

mug

ball

kite

clock

snake

Parents: Naming words are <u>nouns.</u>
Skill: Recognizing nouns

Answers on page 127.

Draw Something

Which word is a naming word? Circle it. Draw it in the box.

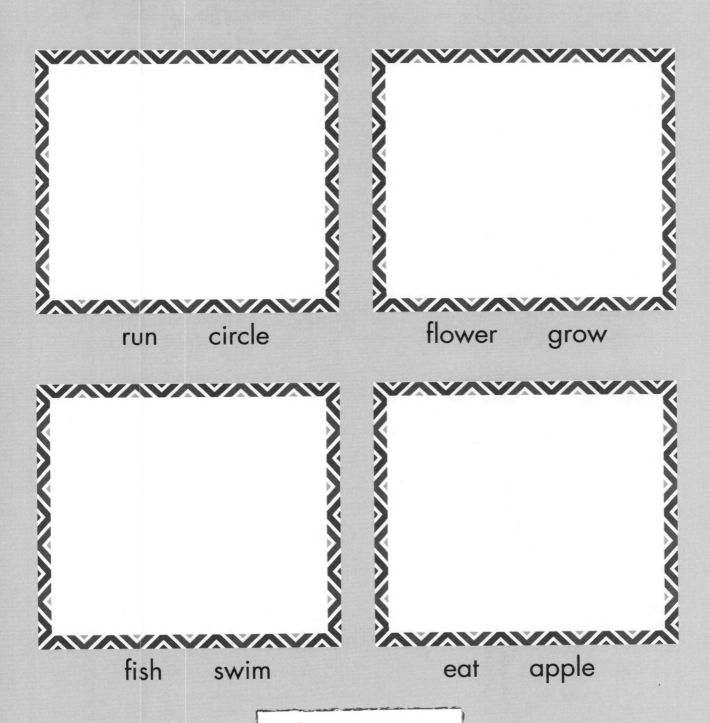

run   circle

flower   grow

fish   swim

eat   apple

Skill: Recognizing nouns

Answers on page 127.

More than One

Some naming words tell about more than one thing. You can add **s** to the end of some words to show more than one.

1 dog   **2 dogs**

Look at the picture. Circle the word that goes with the picture.

   monkeys   monkey

   ducks   duck

   cow   cows

   rabbit   rabbits

   horses   horse

Skill: Recognizing plural nouns

Answers on page 127.

Making More than One

Write an **s** at the end of these words to make them show more than one.

truck__

car__

bike__

train__

plane__

Skills: Recognizing plural nouns; writing **s**

Answers on page 127.

Picture Words

Some words give you a picture of something. They are <u>describing words.</u>

Match the picture with the word that describes it. Choose a word from the word bank to finish the sentence. Cross out the words from the word bank as you use them.

yellow   brown   ~~cold~~   tiny

The snowman is **cold** .

He has _____ eyes.

The clown has _____ pants.

The ants are _____ .

Skill: Recognizing adjectives

100

Answers on page 127.

Feeling Words

Some words tell how you feel. Some feeling words are **happy, sad, mad, scared, excited,** and **tired.**

Draw the face of someone who is feeling **happy.**

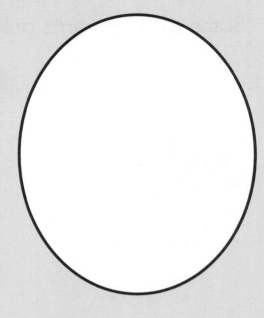

Draw the face of someone who is feeling **sad.**

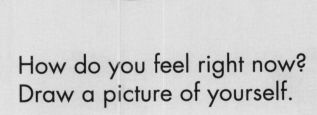

How do you feel right now? Draw a picture of yourself.

Colorful Words

Some picture words are <u>color words.</u>

red

yellow

blue

orange

green

purple

pink

white

black

brown

Read the words. Then color the shapes.

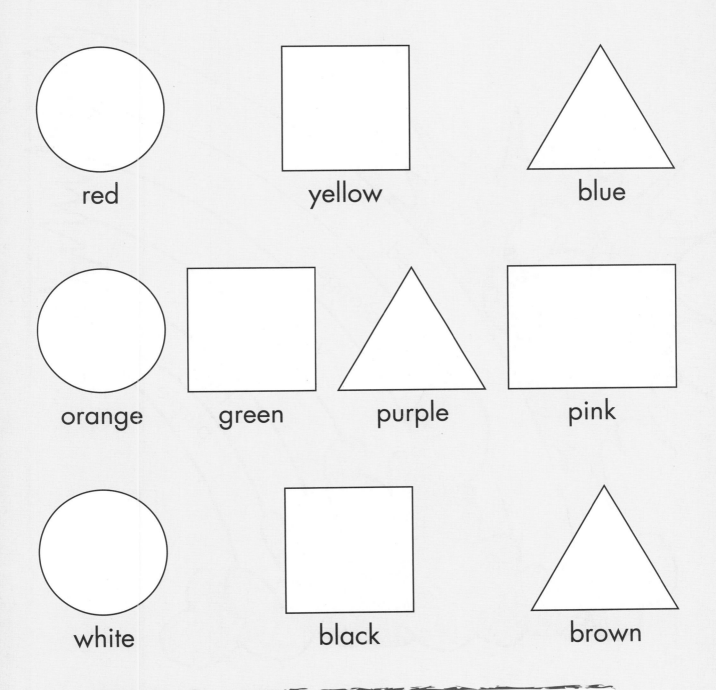

red

yellow

blue

orange

green

purple

pink

white

black

brown

A Rainbow of Colors

Read the words to color the rainbow.

Skill: Recognizing color words

Answers on page 127.

Funny Face

Color in the face of a funny friend.

Color the eyes **green.** Write **green.**

Color the mouth **pink.** Write **pink.**

Color the hair **red.** Write **red.**

Color the nose **blue.** Write **blue.**

What a funny face!

Skills: Recognizing color words; writing color words

Answers on page 127.

Up and Down

U+p spells **up.** Up means <u>toward the top.</u> **D+o+w+n** spells **down.** Down means <u>toward the bottom.</u> These words are <u>opposites.</u>

Some things are found up in the air. Some things are found down on the ground. Circle the things you see in the sky. Write **up** on the line. Put an **X** on the things you see on the ground. Write **down** on the line.

Skills: Recognizing opposites **up** and **down**; writing words

Answers on page 127.

Top and Bottom

T+o+p spells **top.** B+o+t+t+o+m spells **bottom.** Top means there is <u>nothing above it.</u> Bottom means there is <u>nothing below it.</u> **Top** and **bottom** are <u>opposites.</u>

Look at each picture. Read the sentence. Circle **top** or **bottom** to tell where the item is.

Where is the frog?   top   bottom

Where is the worm?   top   bottom

Where are the cups?   top   bottom

Where are the plates?   top   bottom

Where are the shirts?   top   bottom

Where are the socks?   top   bottom

Skill: Recognizing opposites **top** and **bottom**

Over and Under

Over means <u>on top of</u> or <u>above</u> something. **Under** means <u>below</u> something. **Over** and **under** are <u>opposites.</u>

Look at the picture. Write **over** or **under** in the blank to finish the sentence.

The kite glides _____ the treetops.

The airplane flies _____ the clouds.

The bird flies _____ the airplane.

The clouds float _____ the airplane.

Parents: Invite your child to "drive" small toy cars around the room, driving them over and under things. Ask them to tell you when the car is going over something and when it is going under.

Skills: Recognizing opposites **over** and **under**; writing words

108

Answers on page 127.

In and Out

In means <u>inside</u> something. **Out** means <u>outside</u> something.
In and **out** are <u>opposites.</u>

Write **in** or **out** to finish the sentence.

The bird is _____ the nest.

The boy is _____ of the car.

The book is _____ of the backpack.

The dog is _____ the doghouse.

Skills: Recognizing opposites **in** and **out**; writing words

Answers on page 128.

You Can Count on Me

You may know your 1, 2, 3s, but do you know your **one, two, threes**?

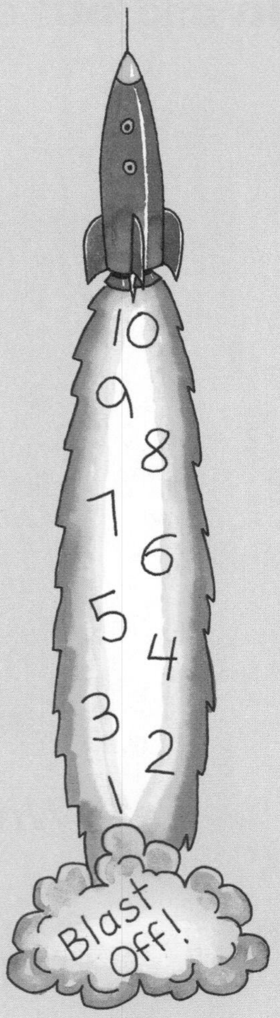

Here are some number words:

1 one ☆

2 two ☆ ☆

3 three ☆ ☆ ☆

4 four ☆ ☆ ☆ ☆

5 five ☆ ☆ ☆ ☆ ☆

6 six ☆ ☆ ☆ ☆ ☆ ☆

7 seven ☆ ☆ ☆ ☆ ☆ ☆ ☆

8 eight ☆ ☆ ☆ ☆ ☆ ☆ ☆ ☆

9 nine ☆ ☆ ☆ ☆ ☆ ☆ ☆ ☆ ☆

10 ten ☆ ☆ ☆ ☆ ☆ ☆ ☆ ☆ ☆ ☆

Blast Off!

Count the number of items in each group.
Circle the correct number word.

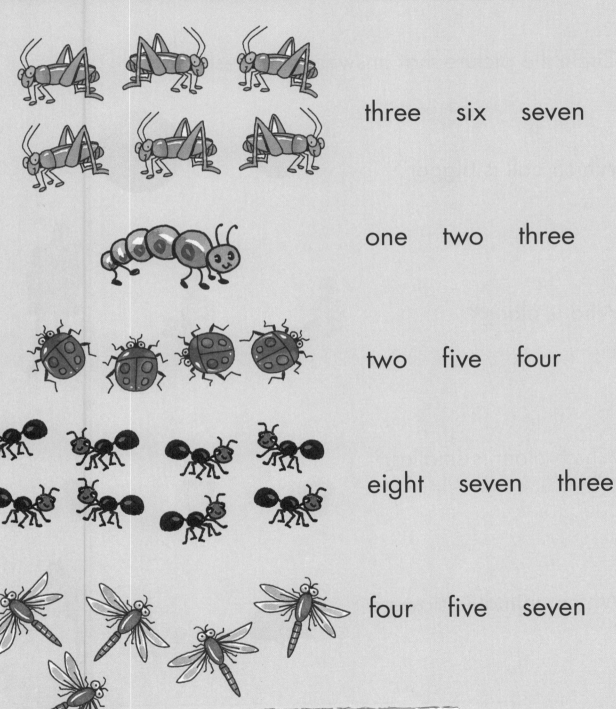

three   six   seven

one   two   three

two   five   four

eight   seven   three

four   five   seven

Skills: Learning number words; counting

Bigger and Biggest

Some word endings help you compare things. These are called <u>comparing words.</u>

Circle the picture that answers the question.

Which ball is big<u>ger</u>?

Who is old<u>est</u>?

Which plant is small<u>est</u>?

Which animal is slow<u>er</u>?

Skill: Learning comparing words that end in **er** and **est**

112

Answers on page 128.

Some, Many, Most

Some words help you compare things.

some	many	most

Read the sentence. Circle the word that tells how many crayons there are.

Laura has some crayons.

David has many crayons.

Pat has the most crayons.

Skill: Learning comparing words
some, many, most

Answers on page 128.

Good, Better, Best

Good, better, and **best** are also comparing words.

| good | better | best |

Read the sentence. Circle the comparing word.

Evan thinks cookies are good.

He thinks cupcakes are better.

He thinks ice cream is the best!

What snack do you like best? Draw it here.

Skill: Learning comparing words **good, better, best**

Answers on page 128.

Right and Left

You have a right hand. You have a right foot.

You have a left hand. You have a left foot.

Left is that way    **Right** is this way

Follow the directions to put each item on the correct side of the page. Draw a line from the item to the hand on the right or the left. The first one is done for you.

Put the pizza on the **right.**   Put the sandwich on the **left.**

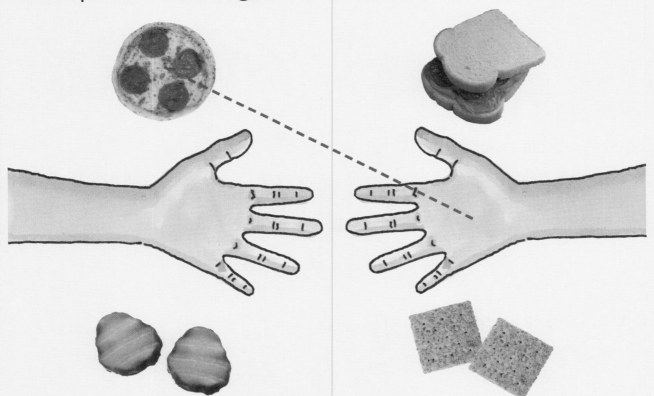

Put the pickles on the **left.**   Put the crackers on the **right.**

Sorting Shapes

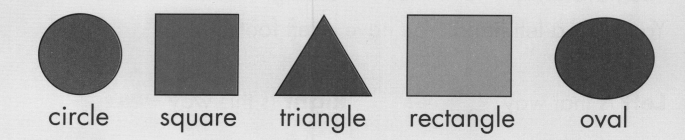

circle   square   triangle   rectangle   oval

Draw these shapes in order from left to right in the boxes below.

oval, square, triangle

square, circle, rectangle

circle, oval, triangle

Skills: Reviewing left to right; identifying shapes; drawing shapes

Answers on page 128.

Reading Left to Right

Just as letters in a word are read left to right, words in a sentence are read left to right.

The seal has shoes.
Draw a line to the seal with shoes.

The fish is pink.
Where is the pink fish?
Draw a line to it.

The boy is reading.
Draw a line to the boy.

Skill: Reading left to right

Answers on page 128.

What Is a Sentence?

A <u>sentence</u> tells a complete thought. All sentences begin with an uppercase letter.

The rocket is going to the moon.

Read the sentence. Circle the word that begins with an uppercase letter.

The bus is yellow.

Smell the flowers.

Lemons taste sour.

My dog is nice.

Skill: Beginning a sentence with an uppercase letter

Answers on page 128.

How Does It End?

Many sentences end with a dot.
The dot is called a <u>period.</u>

Read the sentence. Write a period
at the end of each sentence.
Color the cars on the way up
the roller coaster.

Here we go

I close my eyes

We go up, up, up

They are fun

They go fast

I like roller coasters

Skill: Using a period to end a sentence

Answers on page 128.

119

Who Has a Question?

A <u>question</u> is a sentence that asks something. A question ends with a <u>question mark.</u>

Trace the question mark.
Then write the question mark.

Read the sentences. Put a question mark after the sentences that ask something.

Where are you going

The car is red

When is your birthday

Skill: Using a question mark to end a sentence

120

Answers on page 128.

Simple Sentences

Words in a sentence are separated by a space. Look at the space between the words in this sentence.

The rat is fat.

Copy the sentence here.

_____

. . . .

_____

This is a big pig. Can you write a sentence about it?

_____

. . . .

_____

Parents: Suggest to your child that he or she use the width of their finger to gauge how much space to leave between words.

Skills: Writing sentences; leaving space between words

Answers will vary.   121

Answer Key

page 11

page 14

page 15

page 17

page 18

page 19

page 20

page 21

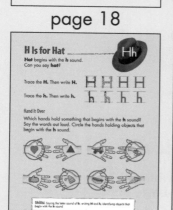

page 22

page 25

page 26

page 27

page 28

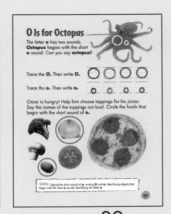

page 29

page 30

page 31

page 32

page 34

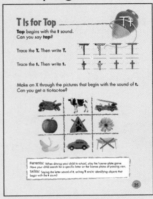

page 35

page 36

page 37

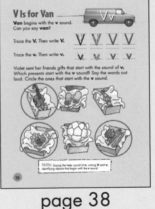

page 38

page 39

page 40

page 41

page 42

page 43

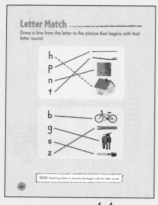

page 44

page 45

page 46

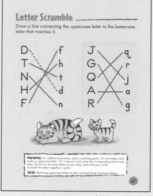

page 47

page 48   page 49

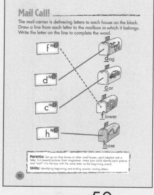

page 50

page 51

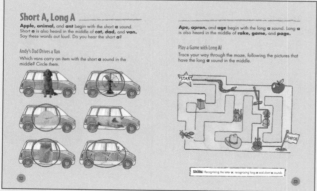

page 52   page 53

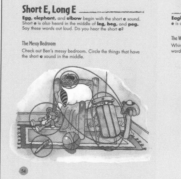

page 54

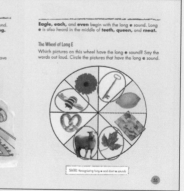

page 55

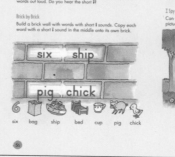

page 56

page 57

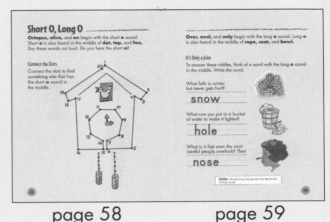

page 58

page 59

page 62

page 63

page 64

page 65

page 66

page 67

page 68

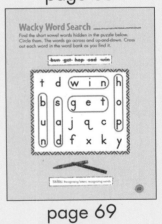

page 69

page 70

page 71

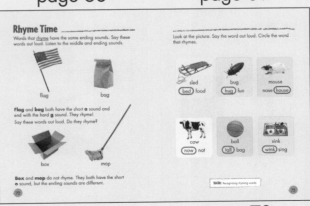

page 72

page 73

page 75

page 76

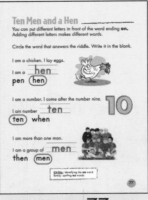

page 77

page 78

page 80

page 81

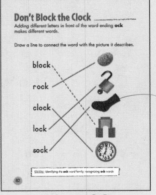

page 82

page 83

page 84

page 85

page 86

page 87

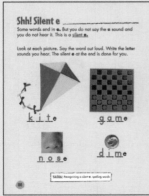

page 88

page 89

page 90

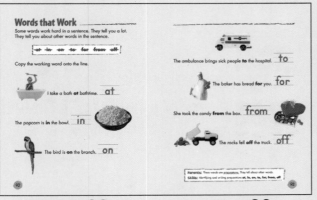

page 92

page 93

page 94

page 95

page 96

page 97

page 98

page 99

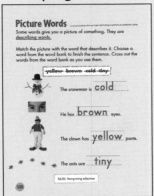

page 100

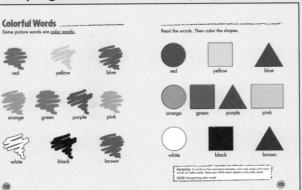

page 102

page 103

page 104

page 105

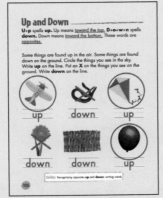

page 106

page 107

page 108

127

page 109

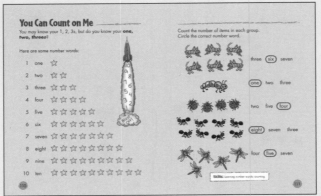

page 110

page 111

page 112

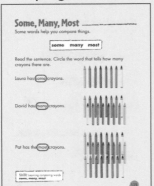

page 113

page 114

page 115

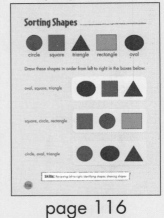

page 116

page 117

page 118

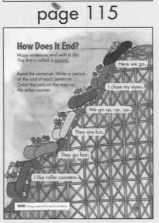

page 119

page 120